feast

feast

east fea

feast

feas

Presented to

_____

On the occasion of

Mops Brunch

_____

From

Mops

_____

Date

May 15, 2003

_____

Feast

Compiled by
Ellyn Sanna

BARBOUR
PUBLISHING, INC.

Published by Barbour Publishing, Inc., P.O. Box 719, Uhrichsville, Ohio 44683
http://www.barbourbooks.com

 Member of the
Evangelical Christian
Publishers Association

Printed in China.

Feast

Be joyful at your Feast. . . .
DEUTERONOMY 16:14 (NIV)

Is there anything better than inviting friends and family into our homes for food and talk and laughter? Those are the times when the warmest memories are formed, the times when we feel truly united with each other. Sharing a meal together means something to us human beings, something that goes far beyond the physical act, into the emotional and spiritual realms.

The early church knew how important eating together was to their spiritual well-being. Acts 2:42 (KJV) says, "And they continued stedfastly in the apostles' doctrine and fellowship, and in breaking of bread, and in prayers." Notice that breaking bread together seems to be as important as praying together—and the fellowship is stressed as much as the doctrine. The New Testament writers remind us again and again that hospitality is an essential part of the church's life.

That doesn't mean, though, that we should feel burdened with one more responsibility in our already busy lives; the Bible doesn't ask us to give extravagant dinner parties to impress our friends and neighbors. No, the word hospitality comes from a root that means "open"—and when we practice biblical hospitality, we will not only open our homes to each other, we will also open our hearts.

For some of us, this may mean we *do* throw extravagant dinner parties (not to impress others but to please them and let them know they are welcome)—but for others of us, this may mean something as simple as sharing coffee with our neighbor or inviting a friend over for take-out pizza. Either way, fancy or simple, we invite others into our homes and hearts; we share our tangible sustenance at the same time we partake of the Spirit that nourishes us all.

Christ Himself knew how important is a shared meal. After all, He chose an ordinary supper to be the symbol of His life and death.

Then at the proper time Jesus and the twelve disciples sat down together at the table. Jesus said, "I have looked forward to this hour with deep longing, anxious to eat this Passover meal with you. . . ."
LUKE 22:14, 15 (NLT)

One

They devoted themselves to. . .fellowship,
to the breaking of bread and to prayer.
ACTS 2:42 (NIV)

Sometimes I tend to have a utilitarian approach to food: My family gets hungry so eventually I feed them. It's one of those never-ending chores in my life, like doing the laundry or sweeping the kitchen floor. I forget that each meal can be a celebration, a time for fellowship and prayer.

My in-laws never forget, though. For them food is more than merely the means to satisfy hunger; it's a sacrament of joy and togetherness and love. Each loaf of crusty bread, each olive gleaming with oil, each strand of sauce-soaked spaghetti speaks to them of family and home, good friends and laughter.

When my husband and I first married, I was surprised to look through his family's photo albums and find picture after picture of the family table loaded with food. Here between pictures of my husband's first birthday was a photo of a table gleaming with china and crystal, dishes of food crowding for space between the candlesticks—and as I turned the pages, watching my husband get older in each picture, I saw the same scene again and again: the same basket spilling over with bread, the same dishes of vegetables and grated cheese and tomato sauce, and at the center the same huge platter; sometimes it held leg of lamb nestled among onions and garlic and carrots, sometimes thick red steaks, sometimes golden chicken or a giant turkey.

"Why does your family take the same picture over and over?" I asked my husband.

He just grinned and shrugged.

When I first visited my in-laws, food seemed to appear out of the kitchen with a magical bounty: Salad would follow lasagna, and just as I was leaning back in my chair, so full I could barely move, out would come a platter of chicken, baked in my mother-in-law's famous bread crumbs. If I tried to venture into the kitchen to see if I could help with the preparation of all this food, my husband's grandmother would push me away, scolding me in Sicilian.

Finally, though, the day came when I was allowed in the kitchen. All day we pared and chopped and grated. I listened to the rise and fall of the women's voices, and their impatient scolding and delighted laughter wrapped around me as warm as a hug.

I learned how to make soup from long green Italian squash, how to fry green beans in garlic and olive oil, and how to stuff manicotti with cheese and egg. They'd been making these same foods for years, I realized as I watched their quick, efficient hands. Their mothers and grandmothers had made these dishes before them, back into the past, and we were part of a long and bountiful chain of food and love.

When at last the table was all set, spread with the feast our hands had prepared, my husband called everyone to the table. I looked at all those bright, beloved faces, and then I turned to the table crowded with steaming dishes. This was something more than a meal, I realized; this was a ceremony of joy. With a heart full of prayer and gratitude, for a moment I wished I could make this shining moment last forever.

But people were already finding their places around the table. "Wait! Wait!" my father-in-law cried.

I met his eyes and smiled. "I'll get the camera."

The ornaments of a house
are the friends who frequent it.
RALPH WALDO EMERSON

Cooking is like love.
It should be entered into with abandon or not at all.
COLETTE

*Music I heard with you
was more than music,
And bread I broke with you
was more than bread.*
CONRAD AIKEN

The test of pleasure is the memory it leaves behind.
JEAN PAUL RICHTER

Green Beans and Garlic

1 lb french-cut green beans
  (fresh, frozen, or canned)
3 minced garlic cloves
½ cup olive oil
salt

Heat olive oil in a large frying pan. Add garlic and cook till transparent. Add green beans and cook till tender. (This will only take a few minutes if you're using canned beans, longer if you're using fresh or frozen.) Add salt to taste.

It is so much more than eating a meal;
it is emotional and bonding, rich and fulfilling.
Sacred even.
JO KADLECEK, *FEAST OF LIFE*

Pasta and Beans

1 lb boneless skinless chicken breast, cut into 1-inch pieces
2 14½-oz cans stewed tomatoes
1 15½-oz can red or white kidney beans, rinsed and drained
1 15-oz can tomato sauce
1 cup water
¼ cup sliced mushrooms
1 medium green bell pepper, chopped
½ cup onion, chopped
½ cup celery, chopped
4 cloves garlic, minced
1 tsp dried Italian seasoning
6 oz uncooked thin spaghetti

Place all the ingredients except the spaghetti into the slow cooker. Cover and cook on low for 4 hours, until vegetables are tender. Raise temperature to high. Stir in spaghetti. Cover. Stir after 10 minutes. Cover and cook for 45 minutes, until pasta is tender. Serves 8.

Squash Soup

1 medium onion, diced
4 large ripe tomatoes
¼ cup olive oil
1 large Italian squash (or zucchini or summer squash)
2 cups of finely cut squash leaves (you can substitute spinach
    or Swiss chard)
2 large finely chopped potatoes
1 cup finely cut green beans (optional)
salt

Heat olive oil in a large kettle. Add onions and cook for 3 minutes. Add other ingredients and enough water to cover everything. Season to taste. Bring to a boil and simmer for 2 hours.

Instead of herds of oxen, endeavor to assemble flocks
of friends about your house.
EPICTETUS

Now and then, I like to make my mother-in-law's food: green beans in garlic and squash soup and pans of lasagna. But the sad truth is I'll never be my mother-in-law. I don't find my daily pleasure in preparing my family's meals. Instead, I find my most consistent delight in writing rather than cooking, and meal preparation still seems like an inconvenient interruption in my day. When I do have to host a family get-together or a gathering of friends, I tend to be tense beforehand, snapping at my children as I scurry around the house, cleaning and cooking.

But a feast, I'm learning, doesn't have to take hours to prepare. It doesn't have to fill the table so full it groans—but it does demand my full attention and presence. A feast means that I set aside my work and preoccupation and join together with others.

Some of our family's best feasts are very simple. Like when my kindergartner and I

Where there's room in the heart, there's room in the house.
DANISH PROVERB

have picnics. We make peanut butter sandwiches, cut them carefully into four triangles each, and then take them to the woods to eat on a flat stone beside the creek. And first we always talk to Jesus, thanking Him for peanut butter and bugs, trees and birds, Daddy and Grandma. Another of our best feasts is when my husband barbecues in the back yard, and we invite our friends up the street to come down and share our food. We crowd around our tipsy picnic table, laughing so hard that the children choke on their hamburgers. The important thing is that we commune together, our hearts open to one another.

But the very best feast is when we come together with our open hearts hushed to partake of an austere and simple meal. A wafer of bread and a single sip of wine give us the most nourishing communion of all.

Hospitality like charity, in order to be true, has to begin at home. . . . Did it count, all this gracious open-house business, if I acted like a hellion the hour before company arrived?

KAREN MAINS,
OPEN HEART, OPEN HOME

Here are some recipes that are good for making ahead o time.

Hot Chicken Salad

4 cups cooked cold chicken, cut up
2 tbsps lemon juice
¾ cup mayonnaise
1 tsp salt
2 cups chopped celery
4 hard-boiled eggs, sliced
¾ cup cream of chicken soup
1 tsp onion, finely minced
2 pimientos, cut finely
1 cup cheese, shredded
1½ cups potato chips, crushed
⅔ cup toasted almonds, finely chopped

Combine all ingredients except for the cheese, potato chips, and almonds. Place in a large rectangular baking dish. Top with the remaining ingredients. Let stand in the refrigerator overnight.

Bake at 400°F for 20 to 25 minutes. Serves 8.

Waldorf Salad

Salad
½ cup grapes
½ cup unpeeled tart apples, cubed
½ cup celery, diced
2 tbsps clear French dressing
Salad greens
2 tbsps walnuts, chopped
⅛ tsp salt

Mustard Mayonnaise
3 tbsps mayonnaise
1 tbsp light cream
⅛ tsp dry mustard

For salad: Cut the grapes in half and remove the seeds. Combine with apples, celery, French dressing, and salt. Toss. Cover and refrigerate for 1 hour. For mayonnaise: Combine all ingredients and mix well. Before serving, gently mix mustard mayonnaise and salad. Serve on salad greens and sprinkle with walnuts. Makes about 2 servings.

There is no greatness where there is not simplicity.
LEO TOLSTOY

Hacienda Brown Rice

1 4-oz can diced green chiles
2 cups raw brown rice, cooked (6 cups cooked)
3 cups sour cream
Salt and pepper
1 lb Monterey Jack cheese, shredded
1 bunch scallions, sliced (including some of the green tops)
6 oz sharp Cheddar cheese, shredded

Spread 2 cups of cooked rice over the
bottom of a greased rectangular baking dish.
Spread 1 cup sour cream over rice and
sprinkle with salt and pepper. Evenly
spread half the chiles, Monterey Jack
cheese, and scallions over the sour
cream. Repeat the layers in the same
order. End with the last third of the rice
and the last cup of sour cream. Sprinkle
with salt and pepper and Cheddar cheese.
Bake at 350°F for 20 minutes. Serves 12.

Citrus Cake

*Nothing
is really work
unless
you'd rather
be doing
something else.*
PETER PAN

Cake
1 19-oz pkg yellow cake mix
1 3¾-oz pkg instant lemon pudding mix
4 eggs
¾ cup water
¾ cup oil

Frosting
1½ cups powdered sugar
2 tbsps butter
⅓ cup concentrated orange juice

Combine all cake ingredients and mix well. Pour into a greased, 10-inch tube pan. Bake at 325°F for 50 minutes. While cake bakes, combine all frosting ingredients in a small bowl. While cake is still hot, spread the frosting over it. Cool cake in the pan. Serves 8 to 10.

Vegetable Stuffed
Pork Chops

4 double pork loin chops, well trimmed
Salt and pepper
1 15¼-oz can corn, drained
1 small onion, chopped
1 green bell pepper, seeded and chopped
1 cup Italian-style seasoned dry bread crumbs
½ cup uncooked, long-grain converted rice
1 8-oz can tomato sauce

Cut a pocket in each pork chop, cutting from the edge nearest the bone. Season pockets lightly with salt and pepper. Combine corn, onion, green pepper, bread crumbs, and rice in a large bowl. Stuff pork chops with the mixture and secure with wooden toothpicks. Add any remaining mixture to the slow cooker. Add stuffed pork chops. Moisten the top of each pork chop with tomato sauce and pour any remaining sauce over the top. Cover and cook on low for 8 to 10 hours. Remove pork chops and place on serving platter. Serve with vegetable-rice mixture. Serves 4.

How to host a feast

• *A potluck* dinner is a good way to get together and share the cost of the food, so that one family doesn't bear the entire expense. My sister has a group of friends with whom she schedules a potluck dinner once a month. They pick a food theme for each occasion and they all take turns hosting the dinner; that way they can count on getting together once a month for fellowship and food—and they all share the time and cost.

• Start a book discussion group and get together once a month for coffee and muffins. The emphasis should be on the books you're reading and the ideas you're exchanging—not on the cleanliness of your house or the fancy food you serve.

• After a Little League game or some school event, why not ask a group of other parents to stop at the local deli, buy a favorite sandwich, and bring it to your house. Cut each sandwich into four quarters and arrange them all on a platter. Serve some chips, raw veggies and dip, and drinks, and you have an inexpensive new tradition.

• Have a spur-of-the-moment, come-as-you-are party. Call up several of your closest friends and say, "Don't change your clothes or put on makeup. Just grab whatever food you have in your refrigerator and come on over right now!" You never know what you'll end up with—and that's half the fun.

•Or you might want to host a "come-as-you-were" party. Everybody should come dressed in the clothes that were popular when they were teenagers—and they can bring with them not only the music that was popular then, but also their favorite foods from their teenage years.

•Have a soup and bread dinner. Borrow a couple of extra crockpots and cook three different kinds of soup. If you have a bread machine as well, your work's all done!

•Have a fondue evening. The butcher will pre-cut meat in small pieces for you to serve on a platter; try beef, chicken, and shrimp, with three or four sauces for dipping. Serve a salad and chunks of crusty bread for dipping in cheese sauce, and for dessert have your guests dip fresh fruits and cubes of angel food cake in chocolate fondue.

Two

I was hungry, and you fed me.
MATTHEW 25:35 (NLT)

When we say we love someone, then we want to express our love with actions as well as words. We give thoughtful gifts, we kiss and hug, we bake cookies and special treats, we serve meals with love and caring.

When we say we love God, we need to also express our love in tangible ways. Obviously, we can't bake Jesus a batch of cookies, though.

Or can we? Jesus said that when we give something to the smallest of His brothers and sisters, we are really giving it to Him. In other words, each meal we serve our family, each get-together with friends and family, each school lunch we pack, we make for Jesus.

But we can't stop there. Jesus wants us to remember our neighbors—the people around us, some of them strangers, who are lonely and needy. The people who may even be annoying and not very attractive. These are the ones with whom Jesus calls us to share our feasts.

I can see Christ's face in the people I love. But He asks me go further and see His face even in the people who are hard to love.

> *How can you love God, whom you do not see, if you do not love your neighbor whom you can see. . .?*
> MOTHER TERESA,
> *BLESSED ARE YOU*

And the third day there was a marriage in Cana of Galilee; and the mother of Jesus was there: And both Jesus was called, and his disciples, to the marriage [feast].

JOHN 2:1–2 (KJV)

A Radically Different Viewpoint

Jesus began his ministry by sharing a meal with these country "nobodies." There is a message in this as we contemplate this scene. Jesus loves these people. The love of God in Jesus is teaching us how we can become who we've always wanted to be because Jesus is "the way, the truth, and the life" (John 14:6, KJV). It is in Jesus that we will be who we've wanted to be. . .by looking into the eyes of Jesus, watching him, and by keeping our eyes on him. As we watch Jesus share a meal with these country men, women, and children, we begin to see as God sees, to value as God values, to pay attention to what God pays attention to, and to love with the love of God. Jesus is showing us the nature of his reign here. At first blush it is plain to see. Jesus thinks plain and simple country peasants are significant, important, and deeply valuable. This unleashes a radically different viewpoint into human consciousness: the viewpoint of God. The Hebrew Scriptures, the Old Testament, is full of direct and indirect references alluding to God's penchant to judge not by appearances but to judge by the heart of a person. God sees the human heart. God knows the human heart. This is the real miracle here, and it occurred during a festival meal.

ROBERT FABING, *REAL FOOD*

Keep on loving each other. . . .
Do not forget to entertain
strangers, for by so doing
some people have entertained
angels without knowing it.
HEBREWS 13:1–2 (NIV)

A Feast of Welcome

Sara called good-bye to her husband as he went off to work, and then turned back to her unpacking. She sucked in a deep breath and tried not to cry. Even though every room was full of boxes, the house looked so empty. But she didn't have time to cry. She had boxes and boxes of clothes and dishes and books to unpack; furniture to arrange; pictures to hang. She didn't have time to be lonely and sad.

But she longed to run next door and talk to her best friend Judy, the way she would have back home. Her heart ached to climb the hill behind their house and visit Grandma Jenkins. She wanted to curl up in her familiar porch swing and talk to Mom and Dad on the phone.

She could call them anyway of course, but it would be long distance now. And she had too much to do anyway.

As the day went by, though, everything seemed to go wrong,

and her heart grew heavier and heavier. Her favorite butter dish had broken during the move. Their green sofa didn't match the blue living room. She couldn't find enough wall space to hang her favorite pictures. None of it would have seemed so bad, she knew, if she just had someone to laugh with over everything; but the house was silent and empty.

At last, in desperation, she called her husband on the phone—and ended up quarreling with him over what to eat for supper. With tears in her eyes she hung up and ran upstairs to change her clothes, then hurried out of the house. She might as well go apply for some jobs today. The unpacking would wait.

Hours later, she came home lonelier and more discouraged than ever. None of the stores in the area were hiring. The fast food places said they preferred to hire teenagers. A woman in an office building had been rude to her. She was hungry and light-headed, and her husband would be home soon—and she hadn't made anything at all for supper. She pulled the car into the unfamiliar street where they now lived; the houses all looked blank and unfriendly, she thought; not cozy and welcoming like their old street. As she parked the car, she could no longer keep back the tears. If only she had a friend nearby.

Blindly, she stumbled up the porch steps. As she put the key in the door, something out of the corner of her eye caught her attention. She stopped and turned around.

There in a neat row along the porch railing were five containers. She took a step closer and peeked inside. A dish that still faintly steamed in the autumn air held a vegetable casserole; a rectangular pan held lasagna; a loaf of bread was snuggled inside a basket; a glass bowl was full of tossed salad; and on the last plate was a pile of brownies, covered with plastic wrap.

Beside the row of food was a large, neatly printed sign, its message followed by five signatures and five addresses. The sign read: WELCOME TO THE NEIGHBORHOOD– FROM YOUR NEW FRIENDS ON THE STREET. COME AND MEET US WHENEVER YOU'RE READY.

Sara wrapped her hands around the warm casserole. She looked down at the street. The houses didn't look so unfriendly after all.

Tips for simple feasts

• **Always** keep a few cake, cookie, and brownie mixes on hand in your cupboard. That way you can invite friends over for dessert at a moment's notice.

Share with God's people. . . . Practice hospitality.
ROMANS 12:13 (NIV)

• Have a game party. This is good if you want to get together with people you really don't know very well yet. The game will keep you busy so there are no awkward silences until you've broken the ice. Serve lots of munchies, and have fun!

• Before you entertain, make a list. Break the work down into manageable chores that you can cross off a day at a time, so you're not overwhelmed.

• After you decide on your menu, make your shopping list. Check what you have on hand already and do the shopping for everything else in one trip, so you don't waste time running back and forth to the grocery store.

•Plan a "make-your-own" pizza party. You supply the crust, and your guests bring their own toppings. Everyone shares the wealth and creates their own pizzas. You can do the same sort of thing with tacos and sundaes, too.

•Use a buffet approach to meals whenever you can. It makes things simpler.

•Host an ice cream party in the summer—and a chili party in the winter. Both arc simple and fun celebrations.

Our life is frittered away
by detail.
Simplify, simplify, simplify.
HENRY DAVID THOREAU

When I open my door, do I send rays to dispel
the night? . . . When I open my heart, does it shine
somewhere like the flame in a cavern, one living pinprick
warding off the monstrous cavity of nothingness?
Am I light in the world, and is this house set on a hill
for the city to see?

KAREN MAINS, *OPEN HEART, OPEN HOME*

We're all so busy, that sometimes it's hard to take the time to
reach out to those around us. All of us are darting around, barely
managing to keep up with the many responsibilities in our lives.
Practicing hospitality seems like too much to ask of us—at least right
now, when our lives are so very busy.

But the Bible doesn't say that hospitality is only for those times
when our lives are calm and well-ordered. (Most of us don't have
very many of those times.) Making a feast for our neighbor, though,
doesn't have to take a lot of time. The point is not to impress or
show how talented we are. The point is simply to show we care.

The following dishes are good to share with new neighbors—
with friends who have a new baby—with church members
who are sick—with anyone to whom you want to say, "I care":

Super Chicken Casserole

4 boneless, skinless chicken breasts, cut into small pieces
½ cup vegetable oil
2 pkgs broccoli
1 cup wild rice, cooked
1 can cream of chicken soup
½ cup mayonnaise
1 tsp lemon juice
½ tsp curry powder
1 cup sharp Cheddar cheese, shredded

Sprinkle chicken with salt and pepper.
Sauté in oil until white. Drain. Cook broccoli. Add rice and layer
with chicken in a greased casserole dish. Stir together remaining
ingredients and add to dish. Sprinkle with cheese. Cover dish with
foil. Bake at 375°F for 30 minutes. Serves 4.

Casserole South of the Border

2 lbs ground beef
1 onion, chopped
1 10-oz can red chili sauce
Pinch salt and garlic salt
2 cans cream of mushroom soup
1 can water
1 can green chili, chopped
1 pkg tortillas
¾ lb cheese, grated

Brown meat and onion. Add chili sauce and salt and simmer until tender. Heat soup, water, and green chili in a saucepan. Line casserole dish with tortillas. Add 1-inch layer of meat then cheese and broken tortilla pieces. Cover with 1 cup soup mixture. Repeat until dish is filled. Top with cheese. Refrigerate overnight. Bake at 350°F for 60 minutes. Serves 8.

Chicken Casserole Family Fare

1 can cream of mushroom soup   1 can cream of chicken soup
½ can of evaporated milk   1⅛ cups instant rice
1 frying chicken, cut up   1 envelope dry onion soup mix

Heat mushroom and chicken soups with milk and stir until smooth. Remove from heat and add uncooked rice. Pour into a rectangular baking dish. Place pieces of chicken on top of rice and sprinkle with dry soup mix. Cover with foil. Bake at 325°F for at least 2 hours.

Broccoli Casserole

2 pkgs chopped broccoli   1 can mushroom soup
1 cup mayonnaise   1 egg, beaten
1 cup Cheddar cheese, grated   Crisp rice cereal

Cook broccoli 6 minutes and then drain. Stir in soup, mayonnaise, egg, and cheese. Place in a casserole dish and top with rice cereal. Bake at 350°F for 30 minutes.

Applesauce Spice Cake

1 cup unsalted butter
1 cup dark brown sugar
1 cup sugar
2 eggs
3 cups flour
1 tbsp baking soda
½ tsp salt

1 tbsp cinnamon
1½ tsps nutmeg
1 tsp ground cloves
2½ cups applesauce
2 tbsps light corn syrup
1 cup raisins
1 cup walnuts, chopped

Cream Cheese Icing
4 ozs cream cheese
1 lb powdered sugar
½ cup unsalted butter

1 tsp vanilla
2 to 3 tsps water

Decoration
1 cup walnuts, chopped
½ cup water
½ tsp granulated ascorbic acid
    (or 2 to 3 vitamin C tablets, crushed)
1 red apple

Beat butter and sugars until light and fluffy. Beat in eggs, one at a time. Mix together flour, soda, salt, and spices. Mix together applesauce and corn syrup. Alternately add dry ingredients and applesauce mixture, beating after each addition. Fold in raisins and nuts. Pour batter into a lined and greased tube pan. Bake at 325°F for 70 to 75 minutes. Cool completely before removing from pan. Wrap in plastic and let stand at room temperature for 24 hours.

For icing: Combine all ingredients and beat until smooth. Spread onto cooled cake. Combine ½ cup water with ascorbic acid. Core apple but do not peel. Cut apple into very thin wedges and drop into ascorbic acid mixture. Blot dry and arrange on top of cake. Decorate the sides with chopped walnuts.

When you give a luncheon or dinner. . . [invite those in need,] and you will be blessed.
LUKE 14:12–14 (NIV)

Cherry Delight

A quick and easy dessert.

1 graham cracker crust, prepared
1 pkg whipped topping mix
1 8-oz pkg cream cheese, softened
1 cup powdered sugar
1 21-oz can cherry pie filling

Press graham cracker crust into the bottom of a rectangular baking pan. Blend together whipped topping mix and cream cheese. Add powdered sugar and pour into cooled crust. Refrigerate for about 10 minutes. Add cherry pie filling. (Blueberry pie filling can be substituted for cherry.)

It is a balanced meal that Jesus serves us, a feast that, in turn, gives us balance to serve others.

Jo Kadlecek,
Feast of Life

Let us put ourselves completely under the power and influence of Jesus, so that He may think with our minds, work with our hands, for we can do all things if His strength is with us.

Our mission is to convey the love of God, who is not a dead but a living God.

MOTHER TERESA,
THE LOVE OF CHRIST

And do not forget to do good and to share with others,
for with such sacrifices God is pleased.
HEBREWS 13:16 (NIV)

[God] never left himself without a witness; there were always his reminders—the kind things he did such as. . .
giving you food and gladness.
ACTS 14:17 (TLB)

Three

Feed my sheep.
JOHN 21:16 (KJV)

All That We Have

When they got home, if they ever did
get home, there would be so much work
to do. Leah shifted her weight and sighed.
Her husband Jacob and their friends
Anna and Benjamin had been listening to
the Man talk all day, but Leah could
barely hear the Man's voice, and she was
too short to even see Him over the crowd.
When she looked up, she saw that Jacob's
face was full of eager light, as though he
were listening to some good news he had
been longing to hear, and she felt a
twinge of envy before her thoughts shifted
back to the meal she would need to prepare when they got home.

With Anna and Benjamin staying with
them, she'd have to find something to eat
besides day-old bread and dry meat, but if
they didn't get home soon, there wouldn't

be time to get the fire going properly, let alone make one of the delicious meals Anna always served when they visited her home. Leah's mind worried the problem back and forth. At least she had packed them all a nice lunch this morning, the bread and fish both fresh and good, but they had eaten their lunches hours ago now, and why, oh why, wouldn't the Man just be quiet so they could all go home and she could prepare her guests a decent meal?

Isaac came dancing through the crowd and interrupted her thoughts. "Mother, I went right up to Him! He smiled at me. Mother, do you—"

"Shh!" Preoccupied, she barely listened to her son's chatter. Maybe the cheese. . .she was thinking, when the crowd began to murmur.

"Did you hear that?" Jacob asked her.

"I can't hear anything," she said crossly. "I don't know how you can. We might as well go home, don't you think?" She looked up at him hopefully.

"They're going to feed us here," Jacob said. "If they can. Everyone is hungry, and His disciples are asking us all to share whatever we have left from our lunches."

"Oh, let's just go home." If they left now, she might have time to make some stew. . .and of course she had the figs. They were good, and Benjamin always praised their fig tree. She caught Anna's eye and smiled. "Are you two ready to go?"

Before Anna could answer, Isaac interrupted. "Mother," he shouted, pulling on her sleeve, "I didn't eat my lunch. I had a stomachache, remember? So I saved it. I was just going to ask you if I could eat it now." He turned to his father. "Can I give it to them?"

Jacob nodded, and Isaac dashed off through the crowd. "Can't we just go home?" Leah whispered to Jacob. "That little bit of food won't do this crowd any good. And I have so much work to do before we can eat. Please. Let's go."

Jacob looked over the peoples' heads toward the Man who stood at their center. "I'd like to think we gave Him whatever we had, Leah. Even if it's only five loaves of bread and a couple of fish."

A hush fell across the crowd, and then everyone sat down.

Isaac wormed his way back to them, his face ablaze with excitement. "They're handing my lunch out to everybody," he cried. "The Man blessed it and now they're passing it out. It's the only food they have."

"How silly," Leah started to say, and then someone handed her a generous portion of bread and fish. She looked down at it; she looked at the bread and fish in the hands of everyone around her; she tasted a bit of the fish and sniffed the bread. It was hers: the same food she had made so carefully this morning. And at last, over the crowd's heads, she caught a glimpse of the Man's face. He looked at her and smiled. She'd been so worried about getting a good meal on the table when all this time. . . . Tears sprang to her eyes.

"I don't understand."

Jacob smiled at her. "I think all we have to do is give Him what we have. The rest is up to Him."

That evening the disciples came to Him and said, "This is a desolate place, and it is getting late. Send the crowds away. . . ."

But Jesus replied, "That isn't necessary—you feed them."

"Impossible!" they exclaimed. "We have only five loaves of bread and two fish!"

"Bring them here," He said. . . . And he took the five loaves and two fish, looked up toward heaven, and asked God's blessing on the food. . . . They all ate as much as they wanted, and they picked up twelve baskets of leftovers. About five thousand men had eaten from those five loaves, in addition to all the women and children!

MATTHEW 14:15–21 (NLT)

*If there's
any at all,
there is enough
to share.*
ELIZABETH MULLENDORE

A Thanksgiving Feast

"*Be nice* to Mr. Benson," Elizabeth's mother told her. "He's lonely."

Elizabeth looked out at the old man on his porch next door. Even from here, she could see the way his mouth made a thin, grouchy line, as though he were so old he'd lost his lips. She frowned. "He's scary."

"He's just old, sweetie. Once upon a time he was little just like you."

Elizabeth looked out the window doubtfully. Mr. Benson was too wrinkly and hunched up to have ever been a little boy.

"Go on out and play," her mother said. "Here's a snack to take with you. And if you get a chance, give Mr. Benson a smile."

Elizabeth took the box of animal crackers her mother handed her and went outside. She put the cookies in her pocket, and began to swing, her back to Mr. Benson. She pumped as high and fast as she could, but she had an itchy spot between her shoulders, as though Mr. Benson's faded blue gaze was tickling her there.

She moved her legs slower and slower, trying to make up her mind to go smile at Mr. Benson. At last, she jumped off the swing set and walked across the yard, scuffing her sneakers in the grass. She came to a halt in front of Mr. Benson's porch and lifted her face, ready to smile.

"Wish I could have some of what you got," he growled.

Elizabeth took a step backward, a little scared. What did she have that Mr. Benson wanted? She looked at his face, and she thought he looked sad, the way she felt when she wanted something so bad she ached, but her mother and father told her no.

Mr. Benson's expression made the scared feeling go away, and she remembered something. She climbed up onto the porch and sat down beside Mr. Benson; then she reached into her pocket. "I'll share," she whispered, holding up the animal crackers.

Mr. Benson stared at the cookies for a moment, and then he let out a funny little bark of laughter. "I meant I wished I had some of your energy, girl." His pale eyes crinkled at the corners. "But I'll take what I can get." Gravely, he reached for an animal cracker.

They sat side by side, eating the cookies slowly, one by one. "This is quite a feast," Mr. Benson said.

"Yes," Elizabeth agreed happily. "Like Thanksgiving."

"Yes." Mr. Benson's voice was croaky, and the word seemed to waver in the middle. "Yes," he said more firmly. "It certainly is."

Elizabeth smiled up at him. For just a moment, behind his wrinkles and brown spots and wispy white hair, she thought she saw a little boy grinning back at her.

Our communities are joyful and creative for me only when I can accept my own imperfections, when I can rush out with my sins of omission and commission and hang them on the cross as I hang out the laundry.

MADELEINE L'ENGLE,
THE IRRATIONAL SEASON

All Kinds of Feasts

I have a confession to make: at first writing this book made me squirm. Like a lot of people, I'd like to do everything perfectly—but cooking is an area where I definitely don't excel. Oh, I like to bake bread and cookies, I like to have a pot of soup simmering on my stove or a kettle of applesauce—but my culinary efforts are sporadic and haphazard. As my family can testify, I'm all too prone to be at my computer all afternoon—until suddenly I realize it's almost seven o'clock, everyone's hungry and grouchy, and our only option is to (quick!) order pizza.

Somehow, though, like most everyone, I've been convinced that feasting and hospitality can only be hosted by people with abundant domestic skills. But if that were true, then obviously lots of the world would be exempt from being hospitable.

Nowhere, though, does the Bible command us to throw elaborate dinner parties in perfectly cleaned homes. Nowhere does it imply that we have to attend the Culinary Institute before we can offer hospitality. What the Bible does say is that we are to offer whatever we have to God and to each other.

If we're domestically skilled and we have time, this might mean we share our wonderful food with everyone around us, welcoming them into our lovely homes. But it might also mean that we take the time to help someone with their computer—or repair their car—or simply listen to them talk. The point is that we share whatever we have, no matter how small or imperfect it might be. Whatever physical, emotional, or spiritual nourishment we find in our lives, we pass along to those around us.

After all there are many kinds of feasts. You might even say that as I write this book, I'm inviting you to my own kind of feast.

Welcome! Enjoy!

Offer hospitality to one another without grumbling.
Each one should use whatever gift he has received
to serve others, faithfully administering God's grace
in its various forms.
1 PETER 4:9–10 (NIV)

*These recipes are good for those days
when you just don't have time to be fancy.*

Lasagna in a Hurry

1 lb ground beef
3 small onions, chopped
2 8-oz cans tomato sauce
1 tsp salt
¼ tsp oregano
¼ tsp basil
Dash pepper

1 clove garlic, minced
1 pkg lasagna noodles
    cooked and drained
1 cup cottage cheese
1 cup sour cream
1½ cups Cheddar cheese, shredded

Brown and drain ground beef. Add onions and cook 2 minutes. Add tomato sauce and seasonings. Cover and simmer 10 to 15 minutes. In a baking dish, alternately layer noodles, cottage cheese, sour cream, and meat mixture. Top with Cheddar cheese. Bake at 350°F for 25 minutes. Serves 6.

Chicken Macaroni Bake

1 can mushrooms
1 can cream of chicken soup
1½ cups cheese, shredded
2 cups elbow macaroni, cooked
2½ cups cooked chicken, diced
1 cup canned peas
¼ tsp thyme
¼ tsp poultry seasoning
Dash paprika
1 tsp soy sauce
½ cup fine bread crumbs, mixed with 1 tbsp butter
¼ cup grated Parmesan cheese

Mix all ingredients except bread crumbs and Parmesan cheese. Pour into a baking dish and top with bread crumbs and Parmesan. Sprinkle with another dash of paprika. Bake at 350°F for 30 minutes. Serves 6.

Muy Pronto

1 lb ground beef
1 onion, chopped
½ cup celery, chopped
1 small can sliced mushrooms
1 can cream of mushroom soup
1 tsp salt
¼ tsp oregano
Dash pepper
1 pkg frozen peas
1 pkg refrigerated biscuits
1 cup Cheddar cheese, shredded

Brown beef, onion, celery, and mushrooms. Drain fat. Stir in soup, seasonings, and peas. Simmer 5 minutes. Pour into a baking dish and top with biscuits and cheese. Bake at 350°F for 20 minutes. Serves 6.

Beef and Macaroni

1 cup elbow macaroni
½ lb ground beef
1 small onion, chopped
½ green pepper, chopped
¼ tsp basil
¼ tsp thyme
1 tsp Worcestershire sauce
1 tsp salt
1 can Cheddar cheese soup

Cook macaroni. Brown meat with onion and pepper. Add seasonings. Combine meat and macaroni in a casserole dish. Pour Cheddar soup over mixture. Bake at 300° for 30 minutes. Serves 6.

*Here are some recipes that can be made on a Saturday
(or whenever you have time) and kept in the freezer
for spur-of-the-moment feasts:*

Turkey Rotini Casserole

1½ lbs ground turkey
1 medium onion, chopped
1 clove garlic, minced
2 8-oz cans tomato sauce
1 28-oz can stewed tomatoes
2 tsp Italian seasoning
¼ tsp salt

¼ tsp pepper
1 pkg frozen chopped spinach,
   thawed
¼ cup grated Parmesan cheese
1 16-oz pkg rotini pasta,
   cooked

Brown turkey, onion, and garlic in a large skillet over medium heat. Move mixture to slow cooker. Stir in tomato sauce, tomatoes, Italian seasoning, salt, and pepper. Cover and cook on low for 7 to 8 hours. Increase heat to high during the last 30 minutes. Stir in spinach, mozzarella, Parmesan, and cooked rotini. Serves 6.

Fresh Apple Cake

2 sticks butter
2 cups flour
1½ cups sugar
2 tsp baking soda
2 tsp cinnamon
3 eggs
4 cups fresh apples, cut up
1 cup nuts, chopped

Mix together all ingredients, beating well. Bake at 350°F in a large baking dish for 1 to 1 ½ hours.

Happy is the house that shelters a friend.
RALPH WALDO EMERSON

Four

"Come and have some breakfast!" Jesus said.
JOHN 21:12 (NLT)

There is an emanation from the heart
in genuine hospitality which cannot be described
but is immediately felt, and puts the stranger
at once at his ease.

WASHINGTON IRVING

A meal is an experience not only of biological food but also
of emotional,

        physiological,

             intellectual, and

                    spiritual food: sustenance.

"Human beings do not live by bread alone" (Matthew 4:4), says
the Lord. . . . A meal is an event for the soul of a person as well as
for the body.

ROBERT FABING,
REAL FOOD

A Feast for the Heart

Jill had tied the shoelaces on her five-year-old daughter's sneakers before she remembered the snow that had fallen the night before. She tugged off the sneakers and went to look for boots and mittens. Before she could find them, though, the baby began to cry and she hurried to pick him up, stumbling over the trail of dolls and stuffed animals that was strewn along the hallway. The house was a mess, her head ached, and she had been up with the baby all night.

"Mom," her son called from upstairs, "I don't have any underwear."

"Why couldn't you have told me sooner?" Jill shouted back. "We're almost ready to walk out the door and now you tell me you don't have underwear?" She sucked in a breath, curbing her frustration. "Hold on. I'll get you some."

Bouncing the baby against her shoulder, she hurried down the stairs to the basement. With one hand, she pawed through the baskets of clean laundry. Finally, she found a pair of boy's underwear in the dryer.

"We're going to be late," her oldest daughter said severely as she came back upstairs. Her daughter picked up her lunch bag from the kitchen table and looked inside. "Mom! You forgot to give me a drink again."

"I'm sorry." Jill put the baby in his infant seat and scrambled through the cupboard, looking for the plastic thermoses. She finally found them in the dishwasher and handed them to her daughter. "Here. Help me fill them."

The baby started to cry.

"We're going to be late," her daughter predicted again.

She was right, Jill saw as she stuffed the baby into his snowsuit and herded the other three children out the door: They were late again, the second time this week. She buckled everyone into their seat belts and car seats, rubbed her aching head, and started the car.

At the school, as she gave out last-minute hugs and kisses, she noticed the peanut butter smeared across her kindergartner's face. "Wait," she said and swiped a finger across her daughter's cheek.

"Oh, Jenny, you were supposed to wash your face after breakfast."

"I forgot," Jenny said serenely while Jill spit on her finger and scraped off the last bit of peanut butter. "And you forgot to look."

Jill watched her children make their way to their separate classrooms. She thought about her house waiting for her, dirty breakfast dishes still spread across the table, each room full of things that needed to be picked up. Her life was out of control. She felt like a failure.

She sighed and picked up the baby carrier. Her stomach growled loudly, and she realized she'd forgotten to eat.

"Sounds like you could use some breakfast. Why don't you come over to my house?"

Jill met the smiling eyes of another mother, a friend of hers. "I shouldn't. . ."

Joy is a net of love by which we can capture souls. . . . God loves the person who gives with joy. Whoever gives with joy gives more.
MOTHER TERESA,
THE LOVE OF CHRIST

"Yes," her friend said, "you should. I can see it in your face."

Fifteen minutes later, Jill leaned back in the kitchen chair. Her friend's house wasn't perfect either, she saw, noticing the piles of old mail on the pantry counter, the dirty dishes in the sink. But somehow the mess didn't bother her here like it did in her own home.

Her friend set a basket of muffins on the table. "I just took an egg casserole out of the freezer. It will take a little while to bake, so help yourself to a muffin while we wait."

They talked as they ate, and slowly Jill felt her headache disappear. They laughed together as they shared their morning trials. While the baby slept peacefully in his carrier, they forgave each other for not being perfect.

"I've got to go home and get busy," Jill said at last. She helped her friend load the dishwasher, and then she got the baby in his snowsuit. "Thank you for. . ." She hesitated in the doorway, searching for the right word. Outside, she realized, the new snow was sparkling in the sun; funny, she hadn't noticed it before. "Thank you for feeding me," she said finally, unable to find a better word.

Her friend's smile told Jill she understood.

Here's a recipe for the muffins Jill and her friend enjoyed:

Oatmeal Muffins

Soak together for 1 hour:
1 cup rolled oats
1 cup buttermilk or sour milk

Cream:
⅓ cup shortening
½ cup brown sugar
1 egg

Add:
1 cup flour
1 tsp baking powder
½ tsp soda
1 tsp salt

Bake at 350°F for 20–25 minutes. Makes 12 muffins.

Sunny Day Casserole

1 jar processed cheese spread, melted (8 oz)
¾ cups milk
4 cups diced potatoes, partially cooked
2 cups diced ham
1 pkg frozen mixed vegetables, thawed (16 oz)
½ cup chopped onion
1 cup shredded Swiss, Cheddar, or Monterey Jack cheese
1 cup round crackers, crumbled

Stir together cheese spread and milk. Add potatoes, ham, vegetables, and onion.

Pour into a medium casserole dish. Cover the dish and bake at 350°F for 45 minutes. Stir occasionally.

Sprinkle cheese and crackers over the top and bake uncovered until cheese melts.

Dixie Casserole

¼ cup butter
¼ cup flour
½ tsp salt
2 cups milk
1 lb cooked sausage (crumbled, or if links, sliced)
1 17-oz can corn, drained
4 hard-boiled eggs, sliced
¾ cup soft bread crumbs
1 tbsp butter, melted

Melt ¼ cup butter in small saucepan. Stir in flour and salt. Add the milk and cook over medium heat, stirring constantly until mixture is thick and bubbly. Continue to cook and stir for 1 to 2 minutes more. Set aside. Lightly brown sausage. Stir together sausage with corn and eggs and prepared sauce in a large bowl. Pour into a small casserole dish. Toss bread crumbs and 1 tbsp melted butter together and sprinkle over casserole. Bake, uncovered, at 350°F for 30 minutes. Serves 6.

Breakfast Pizza

1 6½-oz pkg pizza crust mix
1 lb sausage
1 cup fresh tomatoes, diced (or drained canned tomatoes)
8 oz fresh mushrooms, sliced
1½ cups mozzarella cheese, shredded
1½ cups sharp Cheddar cheese, shredded
4 eggs
Salsa (if desired)

Prepare pizza crust according to package directions and spread dough into a greased rectangular baking dish, covering the bottom and up 2 inches on the sides. Crumble and cook sausage until browned, drain on paper towels. Sprinkle crust with sausage, tomatoes, mushrooms, 1 cup mozzarella cheese, and 1 cup Cheddar cheese. Bake at 350°F for 8 to 10 minutes. Remove from oven. Beat together eggs, salt, and pepper to taste and pour over pizza. Bake for 7 to 9 minutes more. Sprinkle remaining cheeses over pizza as soon as it comes out of the oven. Serve with salsa if desired. Serves 8 to 10.

Breakfast with the Master

One morning a long time ago a group of fishermen sailed home from a long night's work. The night had been dark and cold, and they hadn't caught very much. They were discouraged and frustrated, and they were troubled and confused by the larger events in their lives as well.

When their boat was safely docked, they scrambled off board and made their way wearily up the beach. The early morning sun was glimmering along the horizon, but they were too tired to notice. Instead, they walked with their heads down, grumbling to each other. They could barely face another drab, gray day.

The smell of fried fish made them raise their heads. Ahead of them, they saw a man leaning over a fire. He turned and smiled at them. "Come and eat!" He called.

The Master! They hurried toward Him.

He had made enough for everyone. As they relaxed around the warm fire, eating eagerly with their fingers, they grinned at each other, no longer grumbling. The sun had risen, they noticed, and the water had turned into a sea of diamonds.

Ways to offer morning hospitality

• *Keep* some bagels and muffins on hand in your freezer. That way you're always ready to say, "Why don't you drop over for some coffee and conversation this morning?"

•Be willing to change your schedule sometimes. Spontaneity restores everyone's spirits.

•Freeze some breakfast casseroles to have on hand for more hearty morning meals.

You provide delicious food for me in the presence of my enemies. You have welcomed me as your guest; blessings overflow!
PSALM 23:5 (TLB)

Sausage and Cheese Grits

1 lb mild or hot cooked sausage,
    crumbled and drained
1½ cups grits
2½ cups shredded Cheddar cheese
3 tbsps vegetable oil
1½ cups milk
3 eggs, slightly beaten

Spread crumbled sausage in the bottom of a greased rectangular baking dish. Boil 4 ½ cups water in a large saucepan. Stir in grits and reduce heat. Cook 5 minutes, until thickened. Stir occasionally. Stir in cheese and vegetable oil, stirring until cheese is melted. Mix in milk and eggs. Spread mixture over sausage. Bake, uncovered, at 350°F for 60 minutes or until grits have set. Serves 6 to 8.

Potato and Pork Frittata

3 cups frozen hash brown potatoes (12 oz)
1 tsp Cajun seasoning
4 egg whites
2 eggs
¼ cup milk
1 tsp dry mustard
¼ tsp black pepper
3 cups frozen stir-fry vegetables (10 oz)
⅓ cup water
¾ cup cooked lean pork, chopped
½ cup Cheddar cheese, shredded

Spread potatoes on a greased baking sheet and sprinkle with Cajun seasoning. Bake at 400°F for 15 minutes. Beat together egg whites, eggs, milk, mustard, and pepper. Cook vegetables and water over medium heat for about 5 minutes. Drain. Add pork and potatoes to vegetables and stir. Add egg mixture and sprinkle with cheese. Cook over medium heat for 5 minutes. Then bake in the oven at 350°F for 5 more minutes. Serves 4.

Simple ways to always be prepared to offer hospitality

•**When** you make something like lasagna or stew, always prepare double. That way you'll have plenty of meals in your freezer for unexpected guests–and you can feel free to invite them home with you even on the busiest of days.

•Keep a good supply of snack foods on hand in case someone drops in.

•Keep several plastic laundry bins for when you want to clean the house in a hurry. Papers go in one, clothes in another, toys in another, and so on–and all of them can be carried quickly out of the sight. After your guests leave you can sort through the bins at your leisure.

Our food is to feast our eyes on God. Our meal is to commune with our God. This is the banquet God offers us: real food. This is the banquet meal we are invited to attend forever. This is eternal life.
ROBERT FABING

Five

Jesus replied, "I am the bread of life."
JOHN 6:35 (NLT)

Christ Is Our Feast

So much of Jesus' ministry took place at the dinner table. He began His public life at the wedding feast in Cana; He had dinner with Levi; He fed the five thousand; He ate a Sabbath meal with the scribes and Pharisees; He went home for dinner with Zaccheus; He was eating at a table when the woman washed His feet with her tears and her hair; and He celebrated supper with His disciples on His last night before His death. Apparently, people were so used to sitting down to a meal with Him that after the Resurrection, the disciples on the road to Emmaus were able to recognize Him by the characteristic way He broke the bread.

Sometimes we fall into the habit of thinking of our Christian life in spiritual terms that lack any basis in concrete reality. We forget that Jesus Himself rooted the Kingdom of God firmly in the here and now, the ordinary things we see and touch. He even went so far as to call Himself "Bread."

If He lives in our hearts, then we will always have a feast to share with those around us.

Tips for feasts that focus on celebration rather than perfection:

•*Don't* worry if your house is too small or too cluttered with children's toys. Don't be self-conscious if your furniture is worn or you haven't had a chance to dust this week. The important thing is to open your life to others. Most of your guests won't care if your house looks like something from *Better Homes and Gardens* or not—but they will notice if they feel welcomed and at ease in your home. And they will especially remember if they sensed the Holy Spirit's presence there.

•*Flowers make any meal more festive.*

•Candles create a festive and cozy atmosphere. Besides, the dust isn't visible by candlelight!

•Don't forget to play music at your celebrations. It helps set a joy-ful mood—and it will distract your guests from the pile of unsorted mail on your countertop.

•A wicker basket full of apples, nuts, or citrus fruits makes a nice centerpiece.

•Don't worry if your china and silverware don't match. Some fancy restaurants use unmatched dinnerware patterns on purpose to create a "funky" atmosphere—so why shouldn't you?

•If your guests have young children, think up some activity in another room (for instance, a video in the living room, outdoor games, or art supplies in the basement) that will keep the children busy so the adults can relax and enjoy their conversation.

•No matter what kind of gathering you host, remember that God's Spirit is always your most important Guest.

Here are some favorite recipes for feasts of celebration:

Barbecued Beef Ribs

24 to 36 meaty beef rib bones
1 cup soy sauce
½ cup unsalted butter, melted
3 cloves garlic, minced
2 tbsps onion powder
½ tsp black pepper

Place the ribs in a large heavy plastic bag. Combine other ingredients and pour over ribs. Place bag in a pan in case it leaks. Marinate for 3 hours at room temperature or overnight in the refrigerator. Turn the bag 2 to 3 times. Barbecue over grayed coals for 5 to 10 minutes on each side, until meat is medium-rare. Serves 10 to 12.

Favorite Beef Stew

3 carrots, halved lengthwise,
   then cut into 1-inch pieces
3 sticks celery,
   cut into 1-inch pieces
2 large potatoes, peeled
   and cut into ½-inch pieces
1½ cups onion, chopped
1 bay leaf
¼ cup flour

¾ tsp dried basil leaves
2 lbs lean stewing beef,
   cut into 1-in pieces
1 14½-oz can diced tomatoes
   undrained
1 can beef broth (14 oz)
1½ tbsp Worcestershire sauce
¾ tsp dried thyme leaves

Layer ingredients into slow cooker as follows: carrots, celery, potatoes, onions, garlic, bay leaf, Worcestershire sauce, thyme, basil, ½ tsp pepper, beef, tomatoes with juice, and broth. Cover and cook on low for 8 to 9 hours. Remove beef and vegetables and place in a large serving bowl. Cover to keep warm. Remove and discard bay leaf. Increase heat to high and cover. Mix flour and ½ cup cold water in a small bowl until smooth. Add ½ cup of liquid and mix well. Stir flour mixture into slow cooker. Cover and cook 15 minutes, until thickened. Pour sauce over meat and vegetables and serve immediately. Serves 6 to 8.

Yankee Pot Roast and Vegetables

1 beef chuck pot roast (2½ lbs)
Salt and pepper
3 medium baking potatoes, unpeeled and cut into quarters
2 large carrots, cut into ¾-inch slices
2 sticks celery, cut into ¾-inch slices
1 medium onion, sliced
1 large parsnip, cut into ¾-inch slices
2 bay leaves
1 tsp dried rosemary leaves
½ tsp dried thyme leaves
½ cup beef broth

Trim extra fat from beef and discard. Cut beef into 6 pieces. Sprinkle with salt and pepper. Place vegetables, bay leaves, rosemary, and thyme in slow cooker. Place beef on top of vegetables and pour broth over beef. Cover and cook on low for 8 ½ to 9 hours, until beef is tender. Place beef on serving platter and arrange vegetables around it. Remove and discard bay leaves. Serves 6.

Six

Therefore let us keep the feast.

1 CORINTHIANS 5:8 (KJV)

Portions of heaven are available to us for delightful nourishment in the here and now. In fact we can enjoy [a] feast every day.

JO KADLECEK,
FEAST OF LIFE

A certain man was preparing a great banquet and invited many guests. . . . Then the master told his servant, "Go out to the roads and country lanes and make them come in, so that my house will be full."

LUKE 14:16, 23 (NIV)

A meal is meant to be an event that gives us the human experience of being our true selves in joy.
A meal is meant to re-create us.

ROBERT FABING,
REAL FOOD

Sometimes it's hard to open our hearts to each other. We'd rather keep our emotional doors shut tight, huddling safe inside. But feasts are meant to be shared. You can't eat them all alone.

I walked fast along the beach, tears in my eyes. My husband and I had just had another fight, and I wanted to get as far away as possible from the little cottage we were renting for the week. Life was much easier when I was alone, I told myself, my blood beating hard with anger.

Gradually, the ocean's roar and sigh quieted me. In front of me, the foam glowed white against the blue night that had fallen across the water. I sat on the sand and watched the moon rise out of the ocean, an orange wafer that cast a million dancing streaks. I sighed, feeling a quiet Presence creep into my heart.

The Presence seemed to be nudging me to get up and leave this peaceful, lovely spot. "I don't want to go back," I whispered. "I want to be alone with You." But the gentle Presence insisted, and I got to my feet.

As I drew closer to our cottage, though, I walked slower. I didn't want to go inside. How could my husband and I have gotten to this point, I wondered; how could my lover and my best friend have turned into my enemy? My heart felt as tight as a fist, but I drew in a deep breath and opened the door.

A burst of warmth and light and good smells hit me in the face. The table was spread with food, I saw, and the kids were already sitting down. My husband was at the stove, dishing up the last plate. "You're just in time," he said. His voice was full of apology and welcome.

I couldn't meet his eyes as I sat down; I was still too angry. "What a feast you've made," I said stiffly, looking at the table. As I sat across from him, eating the good food he'd made, listening to our children's voices, I couldn't help but remember another feast.

That day, all our friends and family had shared the food with us. Bright balloons danced in the air behind our chairs, flowers decorated the tables, and I wore a long ivory gown. When my eyes had met my husband's, our gaze was full of promises.

What had changed since then? I looked around the table at our three kids, and my mouth twitched; for one thing, our guests were different today. As I looked at the children's worried faces, though,

I realized that in a sense they were our guests—and what a rude, self-centered hostess I had been lately.

Something was knocking at my heart's closed door, asking patiently to come in. I thought of the quiet Presence I had sought alone beside the ocean; He couldn't live in my heart either, I realized, if I was trying to keep my husband out. I smiled at my children, and my heart began to unfurl. At last, I looked across the table and met my husband's eyes.

His gaze held the same promise it had on our wedding day. And my heart opened wide in welcome.

Here I am! I stand
at the door and knock.
If anyone hears my voice
and opens the door,
I will come in and eat with him,
and he with me.
REVELATION 3:20 (NIV)

While the meal is for nourishment, the dessert is simply for pleasure.
Here is an idea for a great ending to your meal:

Apple Pie

Filling
¾ to 1 cup sugar
2 tbsps flour
1 tsp cinnamon
¼ tsp nutmeg
¼ tsp salt
4 cups apples, sliced
2 tbsps ice water
1 tsp lemon juice
2 tbsps butter

Pastry
2 cups flour
1 tsp salt
¾ cup shortening
¼ cup ice water

Combine sugar, flour, cinnamon, nutmeg, and salt in a large bowl. Add apples and toss to coat well. Set aside.

For pastry: Combine flour and salt in a small bowl. Cut in shortening with a pastry blender or knife until mixture resembles small peas. Sprinkle ice water, 1 tbsp at a time, over flour mixture and mix with a fork until pastry forms a ball. Press dough lightly with fingers only until it is smooth. Roll out half the dough on a floured surface until it is ⅛-inch thick. Place in a 9-inch pie plate.

Fill pastry with apple mixture. Sprinkle with water and lemon juice and dot with butter. Roll out the other half of the dough to ⅛ inch. Moisten the edge of the bottom crust with water and place second crust on top of apple filling. Trim top crust to about 1 inch larger than pie plate. Fold the top crust under the bottom crust edge and seal. Make slits in the top of the pie to allow steam to escape. Sprinkle with sugar or brush with milk. Bake at 450°F for 10 minutes, then at 400°F for 35 to 40 minutes. Serves 6.

*"Blessed are those who
are invited
to the wedding supper
of the Lamb!"*
REVELATION 19:9 (NIV)

None of us ever seem to have enough to go around. If we have enough money to share, then we don't have enough of something else. When it comes to hospitality, we excuse ourselves by saying we don't have room enough in our houses. . .or energy enough after a hard work week. . .or patience enough to deal with people who get on our nerves. Mostly, we just don't have enough time.

But Jesus isn't asking that we only share the things of which we have plenty. He's asking simply that we take whatever we do have, no matter how limited or imperfect it may be, and place it in His hands. We don't have to worry that there won't be enough. He will take care of multiplying our little morsels of time and energy; He will see that there's enough for everyone—including ourselves—with more left over. All we have to do is give it all to Him.

Whether you ever make use of the recipes in this book, never forget—you can still have feasts in your life. All you have to do is open your heart to Christ, offering up to Him whatever you have. It doesn't matter if what you have is perfect or plentiful; all that matters is that you give it to Him, just like the little boy who gave Jesus his bread and fish. He will bless what you give Him, using it to nourish both you and all those around you.

In practical, everyday ways, with our families and friends and neighbors, let us keep the feast of Jesus Christ.

[Jesus] calls us to an eternal banquet
that begins today.
JO KADLECEK,
FEAST OF LIFE

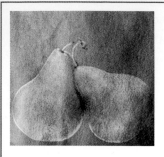

1. BACH: Suite No.3 in 'D', Gavotte 1 (03:45) *Performed by the London Baroque Consort, conducted by André Pavanne*
2. BACH: Suite No.3 in 'D', Gavotte 2 (01:36) *Performed by the London Baroque Consort, conducted by André Pavanne*
3. BACH: Suite No.3 in 'D', The Gigue (02:57) *Performed by the London Baroque Consort, conducted by André Pavanne*
4. MOZART: Flute and Harp Concerto, 1st Movement (10:49) *Performed by the Royal Eltham Symphony Orchestra, conducted by Hilary Scharnhorst*
5. MOZART: Flute and Harp Concerto, Last Movement (08:54) *Performed by the Royal Eltham Symphony Orchestra, conducted by Hilary Scharnhorst*
6. BACH: Brandenburg Concerto No.3, 1st Movement (06:37) *Performed by the London Baroque Consort, conducted by André Pavanne*
7. MOZART: Menuetto from K465 in 'C' major (04:46) *Performed by the Bel Canto Quartet (Leader Antonio Vezey)*
8. BACH: Brandenburg Concerto No.3, 2nd and 3rd Movements (06:49) *Performed by the London Baroque Consort, conducted by André Pavanne*
9. MENDELSSOHN: Andante from Op. 44, No.1 in 'D' major (05:19) *Performed by the Bel Canto Quartet (Leader Antonio Vezey)*
10. MOZART: Divertimento in 'D', 1st Movement (06:18) *Performed by the London Baroque Consort, conducted by André Pavanne*

TOTAL RUNNING TIME: (57:54)

feast feast

east east fea

feast

feas

feast feast
feast
east east fea
feast fea